Rated Я

A Collection of Poems by:
IIII

To the Mouthless

Thank you to Cat for the love and the countless times I wanted to read my poetry to her.

Thank you to Afton, Alex, Amy, Bea, Ben, Bob, Bryan, Caroline, David, Erin, Hannah, Jess, Joel, Matt, Mikey, Paul, Sean, Shannon, and the whole MSMARY crew for listening to me talk about this book for as long as I did.

Thank you to my professors for believing in this project.

Thank you to my family for all the support and love.

Table of Contents

Rated Я

Daddy at work

The Boy Who Could Not Blink

There once was a boy who could not blink.
Well, he could, but when he did, he lost his think.
As a baby, his mother dropped him in the sink.
The boy's head landed with a dink.

So now when the boy did blink,
his mind was erased every single think.
His mental stability began to sink.
By the age of five, all he remembered was the sound dink.

At the age of twelve, he decided not to blink.
He looked real funny the kids used to think.
His eyes wide open like the drain in a sink.
His classmates would spit at his feet, dink dink dink.

By twenty the boy continued not to blink.
It tired him, so his dad began to think
of a device that would never let the eyes sink.
He began to build with metal. It sounded clink.

The machine was designed to prevent blink.
And don't worry, daddy didn't forget to think
about the eyes and how they dry, like soap in the sink.
There is a faucet-like mechanism that makes water dink

on the eyes to simulate a blink.
So though the boy looked crazy, he could think!
People still stared 'cause he looked like a sink.
He walked around, feet heavy, clink clink.

As the boy got older, his life changed in a blink
of an eye. He met a girl who made him think
of love and made his heart sink,
landing on his stomach with a dink.

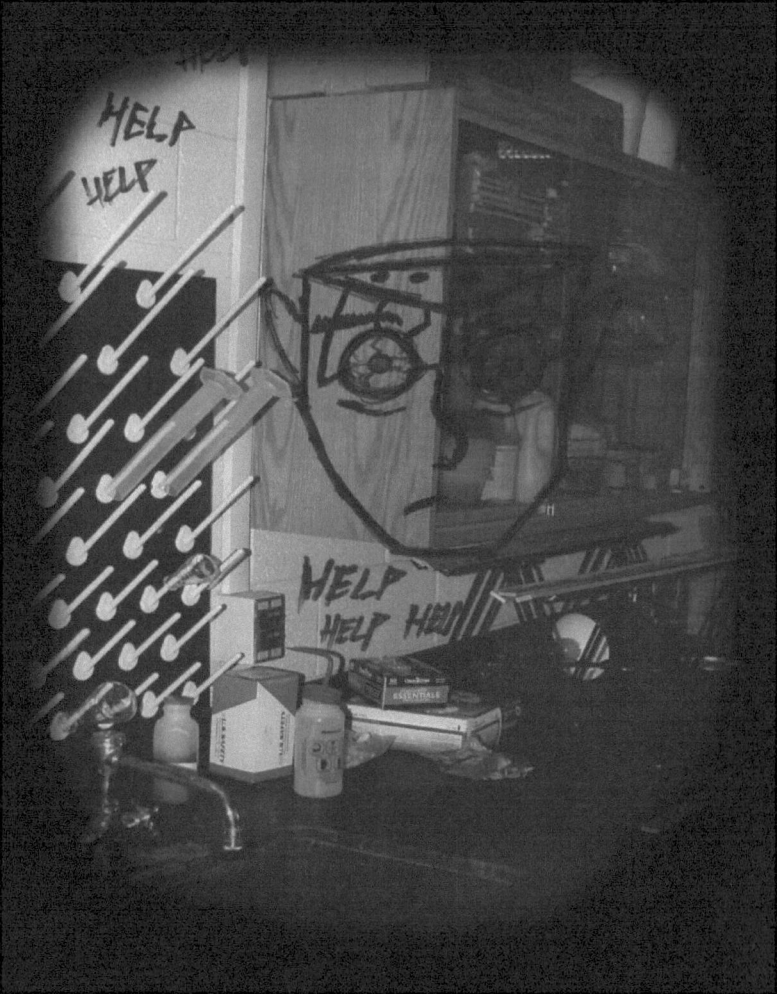

Don't blink

And the girl felt the same for the boy who couldn't blink.
Really, some days, he was all she would think
about, but there was a problem regarding their link.
The girl was allergic to metal, her tears fell, dink dink.

They dated anyway, trying not to think.
Not getting too close, for fear of the girl's health sink.
At first it was just holding hands, fingers linked.
Then sex, without kisses, the bed going dink clink.

But that wasn't enough for the girl, not enough link.
So she thought of a plan. She began to think.
"How do I stop the boy from blinking
without that stupid metal sink?"

It drove her mad. She knew he couldn't blink,
but she wanted him to think
freely, never forgetting, even after a blink.
The girl then had a very horrible think.

His eyelids! She started to think.
She had made a horrific final link.
He can't blink, if they can't sink.
So the girl went to grab a knife from the sink.

She went to his bed, blinking
real fast. He was asleep, eyes open so he could still think.
She brought the knife down, after removing his metal sink,
and chopped off his eyelids, knife going schink.

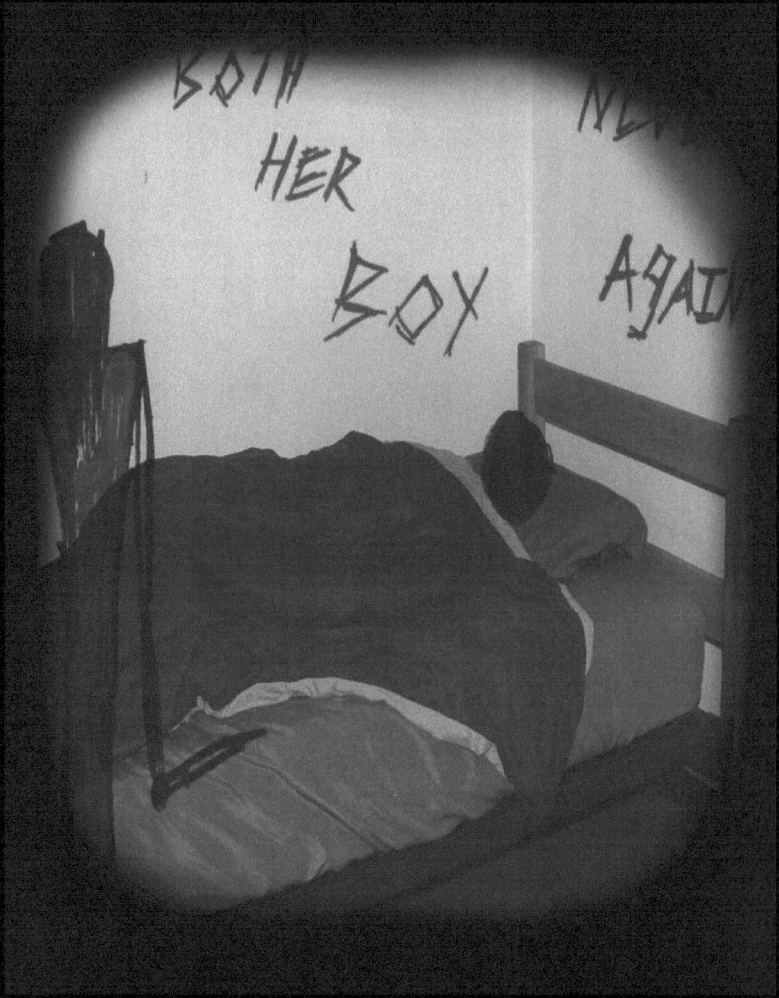

Love is a
powerful thing

She kissed the boy who could no longer blink.
Sadly, though, when the girl removed the metal sink,
she let his eyelids fall. She let them sink.
And so the boy lost all of his think.

All his love of her, gone with a schink.
So the boy, all bloody, had no idea what to think.
He cried, now a baby in the way he thinked.
The girl, clueless of what to do, cried too. She sinked.

Sinked, sinked, sinked and then schinked
her own life away. Never again did the boy or the girl blink.

What is God?

Is Heaven for Real?

There comes a time when we get old
enough to start asking bold
questions

about God, Heaven, and Hell.
So we ask mom 'cause she will tell
the truth.

We ask, "Mom, mom, is God for real?"
She looks at the floor, thinking of the values she instilled
in you.

She knows she will go to Hell,
in her life she wasn't such a swell
person.

She cheated on her LSAT
'cause she wanted a really fat
wallet.

She poked holes on the condom
before she put it on him,
your Dad.

Oh and she likes to steal the neighbor's mail,
looking for pay stubs 'cause the mortgage has failed
to be paid for.

And when your dad went on a business trip,
your mother invited her lawyer friend Chip
over to fuck.

No

The lies she told your dad,
she never really felt bad
for him

or for you. You were just a nuisance.
Really just a waste of two cents
from her paycheck.

And remember when your dad died
from suicide? Well that's a lie.
She killed him.

The gun she shot
was placed in his hand while still hot
to the touch.

She lied to the cops
and you, her stupid cock
of a son,

and got away with it.
So here she is, listening to your shit
of a question.

Now she believes in God and Heaven and Hell.
But honestly, after all she has done, she might as well
stop.

It'd be easier for there to be nothing.
No consequence for something
she did.

So she looks at you and smiles,
looks at you for quite a while,
and says, "No."

Best
friends

Johnny Dew and the Cat

Little Johnny Dew,
all dressed in blue,
made his way down the street.

He saw a cat
so he went and sat
next to its little cat feet.

They always run away,
but this one seemed to stay
for Johnny to snuggle and pet.

The boy felt lucky,
the cat wasn't yucky,
not rotten or decaying yet.

No blood, guts,
or boils filled with puss
to make Johnny feel gross.

Just a dead cat,
a clean one at that,
Johnny hugged the cat real close.

Stay away

Sal the Imaginary Friend

Dear Diary,

I have a pal
whose name is Sal.

My mom says he is fake.
"Let him go for God's sake."
Her words I can't take.
This friendship I won't break.

- Ted

Dear Diary,

Sal and I were playing games
on the street. The kids called us lame.
My mom yelled at us too, she wasn't tame
mannered. "Oh, get rid of… what's his name?"

"Sal, mom." "Sal? Ted, you must find someone real!
Someone who walks, talks, and feels!
Ted, let us pray, pray until
Sal is gone by your own free will."

We prayed at night for hours at end.
We prayed I'd find a real life friend.
One that was real and not pretend.
God, I hope help you'll send.

- Ted

Friendship is
wonderful

Dear Diary,

I met someone not just real to me.
He is a boy that everyone can see.
There is one problem though, a warning I should heed.

Well, his name is Sal too.
Just like my friend who I knew since two.

I haven't introduced them yet.
And I haven't told my mom, heck,
she'll be so happy I bet.
But Sal, he's never liked a soul he's met.

I'll tell Sal about Sal, maybe he won't turn red.
Maybe after all of this, I will have two whole friends!
Good night diary, see you tomorrow at ten.

-    Ted

Dear Diary,

Sal is really, really mad.
My mom is very, very glad.

She still will say, "Get rid of Sal.
Get rid of Sal."

What does she mean when she yells,
"You need to get rid of Sal."
What she means I cannot tell.

Which do I choose?
I guess one will have to lose.

Sal or Sal?

I could get rid of Sal.
Or maybe I should get rid of Sal,
but how?

Sal is always nice to me,
but Sal always seems happy.

Mom says I should get rid of Sal.
"Get rid of Sal," she yells.
I will get rid of Sal.
Shouldn't I only have just one pal?

- Ted

Dear Diary,

I did it! I did the deed!
I killed Sal, even though he began to plead!
I pushed him off the swing.
He broke his neck, I think.

He yelled, yelled as he fell.
Now he's dead and I have one Sal to tell.

All I need is one. Mom was right.
I hope she's okay with my choice tonight.
I had to choose. She'll understand.
I chose the Sal I could most stand.

- Ted

Make a wish...

The Closest Star

You want to catch a shooting star. That has been your dream

for as far as you could think of. Your grandpa has shown

you, countless times, the long streaks of light, the ones so

bright that fly across the night sky. You always wanted to fly,

so you could catch them. And you remember that time where

a star crashed near town, you wanted to go there, but your

grandpa said no. He said you cannot go and steal them from

the ground; you have to retrieve them from the sky while

they are still making that whistling sound. So that's why you

go out every night, even after his death. Tonight, you have

the smell of alcohol on your breath. While looking, you

wander around; you have found a good place to sit. The floor

is cold, but your body is warm. Thoughts begin to form in

your head. What would you wish for? More friends? Or a

way for your life to end? For God to send help for you? In

order for your wish to come true, you must look up at the

stars, not into your mind. Look up.

...before you die

But before you do, notice where you sit, the black road where

cars like to shift left and right. Notice the time, it's the

middle of the night, you probably can't be seen. But wait,

you notice a gleam in your peripheral vision; you must make

a quick decision. The star is close and heading toward you.

Your neck is at a 90 degree angle looking at the star, it looks

like two angels. Yes, you see two shooting stars. Maybe you

can catch both, and they're becoming large. You want to

wish for love, that's what you decide before you realize the

horrible truth. You're on the street. That's your seat and

those aren't stars, it's a car and it cannot see you. You wish

to stay alive, but you don't have much time. The car hits you,

and you die.

Johnny is a
dirty boy

Johnny Dew and his Smell

Little Johnny Dew,
all dressed in blue,
never took a shower.

His body smelled
like oyster shells
that recently turned sour.

Moss grew on his knees,
his finger nails were green,
and mold hid under his clothes.

Flies surrounding the place,
and pimples over his face,
the school kids left him alone.

Oh and don't get me started,
when Johnny Dew farted,
the kids began to run.

Johnny didn't mind,
some other friends he'd find.
He continued to fart for fun.

Octavius
on his
birthday

Sucks to Suck

Octavius was 2,000 years old.
As a vampire, he never died.
As his long life continued to unfold,
he realized he was already dead inside.

He tried many times to kill himself,
to hang, to tan, and to drown.
He'd leave a note on his shelf,
saying sorry for not staying around.

But of course, you know how it goes;
vampires cant die, they live forever.
Octavius knew this too, so
he continued on, depressed, until he met her.

The year was '09 and it was October.
The vamp went towards the hospital to feed.
He picked a window and peered over,
to check if nurses were starting to leave.

Once they were gone, the vamp went ahead
and jumped in, checking his surroundings.
There was a woman lying on the bed,
her breathing sweet sounding.

That mattered not, the man was hungry.
He pushed the sheets past her feet,
her veins began pulsing.
His teeth sank in, blood smoking from heat.

Life is for
the living

The blood gushed from the woman,
spewing into the vamp's mouth.
She suddenly awoke and stared down at him,
looking over her hospital blouse.

"I'm Jane," she exclaimed, "and you?"
"Octavius," he sighed.
The woman looked like she had the flu,
but to him, she looked just fine.

"You're not afraid?" the vamp asked,
"You don't want to run away?"
"No," Jane laughed,
her head and hair began to sway.

She got out of bed and quickly got dressed.
"What are you doing?" the vamp questioned.
"I wanna leave," she started to cover her breast,
"I'm tired of waiting for the end."

The vampire grabbed the girl and flew away
into the night towards his home.
He had started to feel okay,
from that moment, he wouldn't be alone.

They spent months together,
the woman and the vampire.
He started to feel a lot better,
but sadly, happiness often expires.

After some time the woman got more sick,
she never said what she ailed from.
The vamp came up with a fix,
he put some of his blood on her tongue.

Find
something
to live for

She drank it and got real bug- eyed.
Her veins began to glow.
Now as a vampire, she would never die,
at least that's what history showed.

The woman lived, a little sick.
Octavius was still content.
Then he started to feel like shit,
he wondered, did she pass her sickness to him?

He asked her on a foggy night,
"Why were you at the hospital, dear?"
She looked at him sadly and sighed,
"For AIDS, I had AIDS, I fear."

Octavius laughed, "How could this be?
I guess vamps can die if the blood is tainted."
This tragedy came when he was finally happy.
He thought of this when he fainted.

The vampire died that day,
Jane, though depressed, continued to live.
She buried his body with no delay,
it was the least she could give.

Still sick, she thought to herself
how Octavius entered her life.
And how sad it is that he found happiness for himself,
right before the reaper brought his scythe.

But that's how life goes.
It really sucks to suck.
Sometimes life can be so low.
There is no such thing as good luck.

Run child,
the ice man
is near

Beware the Ice Man

In San Fran
there's a man.
There's a van
that you can
buy some ice.
Flavored nice
to entice
all the kids.
Who's to kid?
It is for
so much more.
That bad man
steals his fans,
fills the van,
stuffed like canned
sardine fish.
The kids wish
for an end
with their friends.
No defense
these kids have.
The man's glad.
Has a plan,
it is bad.
He has planned
to now cook,
do not look,
all the kids

in a pan
so he can
make them melt.
Make them yell
as the flames
melt their brains.
Liquid now,
smoke around.
The ice man,
glad he can
do this feat,
pulls out sheets.
Metal clink,
sounds like dink.
Liquid poured,
he is sure
as they freeze
they will please
other kids
in his biz.
Freezer closed,
the van cold.
Ice is made
from kid brain.
Now you know.
Too late though.
All the kids
are now his.

Searching
for a snack

Johnny Dew Picks his Nose

Little Johnny Dew,
all dressed in blue,
went to pick his nose.

He loved to keep,
and also eat,
the treasure it enclosed.

He picked and picked
until he pricked,
and his nose started to bleed.

But he didn't care,
he went back in there,
his hunger he wanted to feed.

The kids make fun,
Johnny feels shunned,
about the things he loves.

This boy isn't lame,
you all do the same,
so who are you to judge?

bugs are people too

A Bug's Life

My name is Annie
and I'm twelve years old.
Let me tell you a story,
it's one I've never told.

I have a passion
that makes me feel free.
That passion is bugs,
I've loved them since three.

Some find them gross.
Some find them annoying.
I find them beautiful,
and simply mind-blowing.

Humans can be so mean.
There is hate and no love.
So at ten I prayed
to become a small bug.

At first nothing happened.
I'd cry at dinner most nights.
I hated being human.
So much darkness and no light.

After meals, I'd be hungry
from crying in my seat.
I'd eat only ice cream.
"Annie, you are what you eat."

My brother screamed this
all out of the blue.
If this was factual,
my dream could come true.

Not for human
consumption

I rushed out the house
with a smile on my face,
and saw a spider
in its home, its space.

I felt bad for the bug,
but I needed to change.
I needed to eat it
so DNA would rearrange.

It tasted bad,
real bad in fact,
but I ate it,
saving the head for last.

Spider puss oozed on my hand
as I stared at the eyes.
That wasn't the last consumed.
Next were moths and then flies.

But the day that changed me,
the one that makes the tale,
was when I ate the mosquito,
dead in the corner, all stale.

So far I hadn't changed,
but I liked the taste of bugs,
when I bit the needle fly,
I saw a squirt of red blood.

It meant nothing to me,
at least, not at first,
but then something happened,
it was my brother's curse.

You are what
you eat

I was in the forest
collecting butterflies,
and then I felt something.
It felt wet and it hurt inside.

I looked down to see
red clumped on my shorts.
I screamed, "What is this?
Why am I sore?"

I unbuttoned my bottoms,
and looked at my panties.
There was blood, really red,
like cherry candies.

Remember the mosquito?
and how it had bled.
"You are what you eat."
That's what my brother said.

Are you okay?

Smile they Say

Smile they say
The village doesn't frown
Smile they say
You'll be thrown out of town

Smile they say
Emotions aren't allowed
Smile they say
Don't spread sadness around

Smile they say
But what if you are sad?
Smile they say
What makes a frown so bad?

Smile they say
Not as fine as you seem
Smile they say
You need to let off some steam

Smile they say
But sadly you can't cry
Smile they say
Sometimes you wish to die

Smile they say
If you don't stop frowning
Smile they say
They will send you drowning

Smile they say
Or maybe they'll do worse
Smile they say
They will cut your lips first

The
people of
the village

Smile they say
Then they'll break your teeth
Smile they say
Your gums, they'll put a leach

Smile they say
But they will keep your tongue
Smile they say
So you can taste the blood

Smile they say
They will bring out stiches
Smile they say
All those bastard witches.

Smile they say
But you choose not to be
Smile they say
Like the community

Smile they say
So I don't feel so bad
Smile they say
For you, my stupid lad

Smile they say
They'll remove your whole mouth
Smile they say
Then you'll be moved down south

Smile they say
With the rest of your kind
Smile they say
All the mouthless you'll find

The
Mouthless

Smile they say
Now this is your new home
Feeling *they* say
You're no longer alone

Mystery
Box

Johnny Dew and his Box

Little Johnny Dew,
all dressed in blue,
always carried a box.

Questioned all day,
Johnny would say,
he hated the feeling of socks.

The box would smell.
You couldn't tell
what was in that cube.

The box looked damp,
and as a matter of fact,
it smelled a little like lube.

One day the box dropped,
and cum spilled out slop,
tainting all inside.

He kept his sperm,
well past its term,
for his future bride.

Don't look
behind you

To whom it may concern

This book is mine.
Don't be mistaken,
you may have paid the fine,
but I, I have spent the time.

You paid for my book,
at least you should have.
Some of you are crooks,
a matter I won't overlook.

I worked hard on this lore,
countless days writing and drawing.
If this book you did not pay for,
I will make you feel sore.

First, realize that you are not safe.
You hold my weapon in your hands.
These pages could be laced
with poison from a foreign place.

Or I could be near you,
ready to grab these very pages.
I'd smash the corner right into
your eyes, bruising them blue.

Or there is my favorite method,
I will kill you with words.
In my poems you have accepted
the gross and the unexpected.

You will contemplate life from here on.
Everything I want questioned.
What is true in these poem-songs,
isn't going to be for every person.

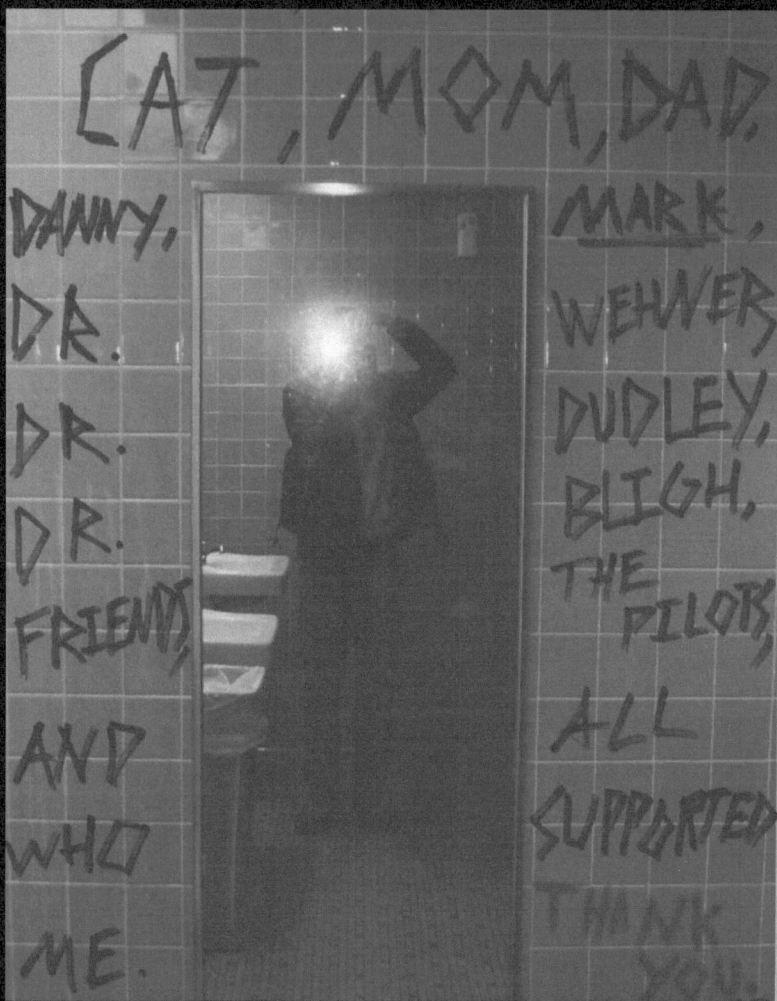

For the crooks that stole this:
I hope Johnny Dew haunts your dreams,
and the ice man turns your kids to icy bliss,
and Jane scares you with a hiss.

Your star comes crashing down
all over your mouthless town you live in,
and you can no longer blink, don't frown,
until mosquito Annie bites you all around.

I hope you find that your mother lies,
and your imaginary friend kills you.
Wait, wait, I'm sorry these words are a crime.
Even if you stole these poems, enjoy your time.

III

www.ingramcontent.com/pod-product-compliance
Lightning Source LLC
LaVergne TN
LVHW010030070426
835508LV00005B/288